# TIME-HONORED TRADITIONS

*Replicate Classic Quilts of Centuries Past*

✦✦✦✦✦✦✦✦✦✦✦✦✦✦✦✦✦✦✦✦✦✦✦✦

## Annette Plog

Martingale
Create with Confidence

Time-Honored Traditions:
Replicate Classic Quilts of Centuries Past
© 2021 by Annette Plog

Martingale®
18939 120th Ave. NE, Ste. 101
Bothell, WA 98011-9511 USA
ShopMartingale.com

Printed in Hong Kong
26 25 24 23 22 21          8 7 6 5 4 3 2 1

Library of Congress Cataloging-in-Publication Data is available upon request.

ISBN: 978-1-68356-092-0

## MISSION STATEMENT

We empower makers who use fabric and yarn
to make life more enjoyable.

## CREDITS

PUBLISHER AND
CHIEF VISIONARY OFFICER
Jennifer Erbe Keltner

CONTENT DIRECTOR
Karen Costello Soltys

DESIGN MANAGER
Adrienne Smitke

MANAGING EDITOR
Tina Cook

PRODUCTION MANAGER
Regina Girard

ACQUISITIONS AND
DEVELOPMENT EDITOR
Laurie Baker

BOOK DESIGNER
Angie Haupert Hoogensen

TECHNICAL EDITOR
Carolyn Beam

PHOTOGRAPHERS
Adam Albright
Brent Kane

COPY EDITOR
Sheila Chapman Ryan

ILLUSTRATOR
Lisa Lauch

SPECIAL THANKS
*Photography for this book was taken at the home of
Lianne Anderson of Arlington, Washington.*

## DEDICATION

*To my supportive and long-suffering husband, Jim;
my children, Lauren and David; their spouses, Clay and
Alyson; and my grandchildren, Lucy, Joshua, and Riley.
Thank you all for your inspiration, support, and
encouragement. You are the loves of my life and
I could not have done this without you all!*

# Contents

# Introduction

I've always loved scrappy quilts. They tell a story that's reflected in the fabrics. When I started quilting, I wanted to re-create antique quilts, which required collecting traditional fabrics similar to those in the original quilts. Over the years I've developed a curated stash of traditional fabrics that allows me to easily reproduce the look I love.

To help you choose fabrics for the reproduction quilts in this book, sample swatches are included in "The Care and Feeding of a Fabric Stash" on page 6. From Lancaster blue to poison green to a simple shirting, each fabric has a distinct color and print. By examining the sample swatches, you'll be able to recognize the specific fabrics that will help you build your stash and achieve authentic-looking quilts from the past. Once you've added the base fabrics to your stash, choosing additional fabrics will help your stash grow and reflect your own personality. Questions about how much to buy and how to store your fabrics are also answered in this chapter.

I want to encourage you to stretch your quilting boundaries and try new colors and prints. Each chapter of this book introduces a quilt project, and most include sewing tips for making that project, as well as history about the fabrics used. Working through the information, whether you choose to make the project quilts or not, will help you re-create the looks *you* love.

# The Care and Feeding of a Fabric Stash

*A well-curated stash is a scrap quilter's best friend. Having lots of beautiful fabrics at your fingertips is helpful when the creative juices are flowing—no need to stop sewing to run to the quilt shop.*

If you're not sure how to start a well-balanced stash of reproduction fabrics, let me help! Frequently quilters ask me what fabrics to buy or how to organize their fabrics. Although there are no correct answers to these questions, you'll find guidelines in this chapter that can help you make the best decisions for developing your personal stash.

## how do I organize my fabric?

Everyone has ideas about how to arrange fabrics for maximum efficiency. I sort my fabrics by size and color. I put ¼-yard to 3-yard cuts on shelves, sorted by color. Anything smaller than ¼ yard goes in the scrap basket. Anything greater than 3 yards I store in a different location, which makes it easier to find the larger yardages when I'm looking for fabric for sashing, borders, and backings. Also, by segregating the larger pieces, I'm less likely to accidentally cut into a large piece that was bought for a specific purpose.

Just like the kitchen pantry, it's helpful to refill your stash as you use it up. If all your indigos are used in a specific project, look for the next new line of fabric featuring indigos and purchase more when you see them. You'll develop a scrappy, curated stash if you collect fabrics that you love and replace them after they're used. Choosing your favorite fabrics will allow your creativity to bloom. Surround yourself with fabrics that inspire you and you'll enjoy every minute of your time sewing!

## what fabrics should I buy?

I have a large stash of traditional fabrics. My fabrics run from large chintz florals to small calico prints. There are perennial items that belong in every traditional fabric stash. Starting on page 7 you'll find my recommended fabrics by color and type that will help the beginning fabric collector get started.

## REDS

Have a variety! *Turkey red* (left) is a bright red with mostly green, yellow, and blue figures in the print. *Madder red* (center) is also a bright red, but traditionally the color faded to a reddish-brown. This faded reddish-brown is what reproduction fabrics imitate. *Clarets* (right) are wine-colored red fabrics that were popular in the late 1800s.

## CHROME YELLOWS

*Chrome yellow* is a clean, clear yellow fabric, usually with a small print, that was originally made with a mineral dye. The fabric is bright and brilliant.

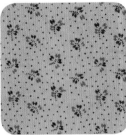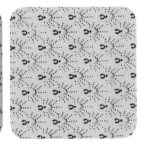

## POISON GREENS

The term *poison green* comes from the early use of arsenic in the dye. It indicates a deep emerald fabric, often with yellow, red, or black colors in the print.

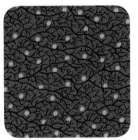

## GOLDS

*Chrome orange* (left and right), or cheddar, is a deep orange fabric, sometimes with a small navy or black print. *California gold* (center) is a soft butterscotch color.

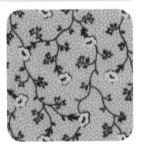

## PRUSSIAN BLUES

*Prussian blue* is a deep blue fabric popular in the 1840s and 1850s. The dye was originally discovered by a German scientist. Compare Prussian blue to *Lancaster blue* (page 8) and *indigo* (page 9).

## PURPLES

Choose purple or mauve fabrics that are medium in value and feature small-scale light or dark printing. A stable purple dye for cottons wasn't discovered until late in the 1800s.

## DOUBLE PINKS

*Double pinks* have a medium pink base featuring either a darker pink print or a small white dot. They are also called *cinnamon pinks*.

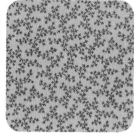

## LANCASTER BLUES

A medium blue background with a darker blue print, *Lancaster blue* is also called *double blue*. The fabric is commonly found in quilts from Pennsylvania.

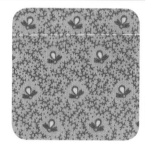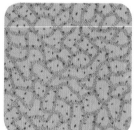

## MOURNING PRINTS

Dark gray, purple, indigo, or black fabric that features a light print are known as *mourning prints*. They became popular in the late 1800s, when fashion dictated that a widow wear all black for a year and a day. For at least six months after that, half of the clothing she was wearing could be prints such as these.

## BROWNS

Have a variety of browns on hand, including *madder brown* (left), a coppery brown fabric; *chocolate* (center), a very dark brown; as well as soft medium to light tans (right). Brown fabrics are an invaluable addition to scrappy quilts.

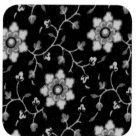

## INDIGOS

A dark blue that's almost black, *indigo* is commonly printed with a white or light motif. Indigo was one of the earliest dependable dyes and was very popular among quilters.

## SHIRTINGS

Most shirtings have a white or cream background with small brown, black, red, or blue prints. They provide great contrast with darker fabrics. In short, they're the perfect light fabric.

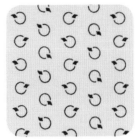

## STRIPES

Collect narrow to wide stripes in a variety of colors. Striped fabrics may be woven (right), where each thread is dyed before being woven together to make fabric, or printed, where the pattern is printed on already woven fabric (left and center).

## CHINTZES

Chintz fabrics were very popular in the early 1800s. Originally from Europe or Asia, chintz cottons were often block printed or painted and had a shiny glaze to the fabric. The floral print was usually large and sparse with the background showing between the motifs. Collect small to large florals on a variety of colored backgrounds.

# Indigo Puzzle Box

*Who doesn't love a blue quilt? The antique quilt that inspired my version has that classic blue-and-light combination that I find irresistible. I asked my block exchange group to help reproduce the antique pattern and they rose to the challenge. The contrast in values is striking and never fails to delight!*

## materials

*Yardage is based on 42"-wide fabric.*

⅓ yard *each* of 10 assorted navy prints for blocks

¼ yard *each* of 10 assorted cream prints for blocks

4¾ yards of cream-and-blue print for setting pieces, outer border, and binding

⅔ yard of navy print for inner border

7⅛ yards of fabric for backing

85" × 101" piece of batting

## cutting

*All measurements include ¼"-wide seam allowances.*

**From *each* of the navy prints, cut:**

✦ 4 squares, 4½" × 4½"; cut in half diagonally to yield 8 large triangles (80 total)

✦ 2 squares, 3⅞" × 3⅞" (20 total)

✦ 8 squares, 3¼" × 3¼" (80 total)

✦ 8 squares, 2¾" × 2¾" (80 total)

**From *each* of the cream prints, cut:**

✦ 4 squares, 3½" × 3½"; cut in half diagonally to yield 8 small triangles (80 total)

✦ 8 squares, 3¼" × 3¼" (80 total)

✦ 8 squares, 2¾" × 2¾" (80 total)

**From the cream-and-blue print, cut:**

✦ 2 strips, 17¼" × 42"; crosscut into 4 squares, 17¼" × 17¼". Cut the squares into quarters diagonally to yield 16 side setting triangles (2 will be extra).

✦ 4 strips, 11¾" × 42"; crosscut into 12 setting squares, 11¾" × 11¾"

✦ 9 strips, 4½" × 42"

✦ 9 strips, 2½" × 42"

✦ 2 squares, 9" × 9"; cut in half diagonally to yield 4 corner setting triangles

**From the navy print for inner border, cut:**

✦ 8 strips, 2½" × 42"

PIECED BY
Annette Plog
MACHINE
QUILTED BY
Sheri Mecom
♦♦♦
FINISHED QUILT
76¼" × 92¼"
FINISHED BLOCK
11¼" × 11¼"

# making the blocks

Use a ¼" seam allowance. Press all seam allowances as indicated by the arrows in the illustrations.

1 For one block, select one 3⅞" square and four 2¾" squares from one navy print; four large triangles and four 3¼" squares from a second navy print; and four small triangles, four 3¼" squares, and four 2¾" squares from one cream print.

2 Sew small cream triangles to opposite edges of the navy 3⅞" square. Sew small cream triangles to the remaining edges. Trim the unit to measure 5¼" square, including seam allowances.

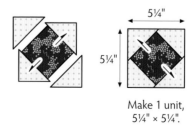

Make 1 unit,
5¼" × 5¼".

3 Sew the large navy triangles to the step 2 unit in the same manner to complete the center unit. Trim the unit to 7¼" square, including seam allowances.

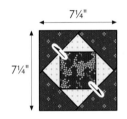

Make 1 unit,
7¼" × 7¼".

4 Draw a diagonal line from corner to corner on the wrong side of a cream 3¼" square and layer it on top of a navy 3¼" square, right sides together. Sew ¼" from both sides of the drawn line. Cut on the line to yield two half-square-triangle units. Trim each unit to 2¾" square, including seam allowances. Repeat to make a total of eight units.

Make 8 units,
2¾" × 2¾".

5 Sew half-square-triangle units to opposite edges of a cream 2¾" square. Repeat to make four side units. Each unit should measure 2¾" × 7¼", including seam allowances.

Make 4 side units,
2¾" × 7¼".

6 Sew side units to opposite edges of the center unit. Add a navy 2¾" square to each end of the remaining two side units. Join these units to the top and bottom of the center unit to complete the block, which should measure 11¾" square, including seam allowances. Repeat to make a total of 20 blocks.

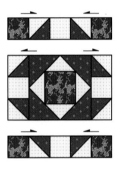
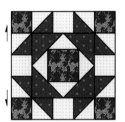

Make 20 blocks,
11¾" × 11¾".

## BLUE GOLD

*Most associated with dark blue jeans, indigo can range from light sky blue to deep navy. While today's dyes are mostly synthetic, natural indigo dye derived from tropical plants has been used for textiles and printing for centuries. Once Vasco da Gama discovered a sea route to India, indigo became a valued import to the west and earned the nickname "blue gold."*

# assembling the quilt top

1 Refer to the quilt assembly diagram below to arrange the blocks and the cream-and-blue setting triangles and squares in eight diagonal rows. Sew the blocks, squares, and side triangles together in each row. Join the rows. Add the corner triangles last. The quilt center should measure 64¼" × 80¼", including seam allowances.

2 Join the navy 2½" × 42" strips end to end to make one long strip. From the pieced strip, cut two 2½" × 80¼" strips and two 2½" × 68¼" strips for the inner border. Sew the 80¼"-long strips to opposite sides of the quilt center. Sew the 68¼"-long strips to the top and bottom. The quilt top should measure 68¼" × 84¼", including seam allowances.

Quilt assembly

3 Join the cream-and-blue 4½" × 42" strips end to end to make one long strip. From the pieced strip, cut two 4½" × 84¼" strips and two 4½" × 76¼" strips for the outer border. Sew the 84¼"-long strips to opposite sides of the quilt top. Sew the 76¼"-long strips to the top and bottom. The quilt top should measure 76¼" × 92¼".

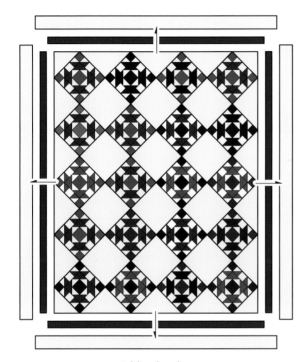

Adding borders

# finishing the quilt

For help with any of the following finishing steps, visit ShopMartingale.com/HowtoQuilt for downloadable instructions.

1 Layer the quilt top, batting, and backing. Baste the layers together.

2 Quilt by hand or machine. The quilt shown is machine quilted using an interlocking feather pattern.

3 Use the cream-and-blue 2½"-wide strips to make the binding; attach the binding to the quilt.

## STOP THE BLEEDING!

*Do you prewash your quilting fabrics? Dyes can run and bleed when the fabric color is dark and intense. The worst offenders are indigo, navy, deep red, purple, and green. It's ideal to prewash darker fabrics and set the color before using them in a quilt. Adding vinegar or products designed to set fabric dyes in the washer is a good start. After the quilt is finished, I give it a good rinse using a color-catching sheet to catch any dyes that might still migrate. For a project like Indigo Puzzle Box, prewashing your indigo fabrics prior to cutting will help ensure that the blue dyes don't bleed onto the cream prints once the top is completed.*

# Garden Path Table Topper

*Here's your opportunity to reach into your stash and pull out your loveliest red fabrics. I've used different red fabrics, from small prints to sweet red checks. I also varied the light fabrics from cream to tan. This makes each block different, but they blend together nicely. I've been told that all reds go together, so make this quilt as scrappy as you want!*

## materials

*Yardage is based on 42"-wide fabric.*

¾ yard *total* of assorted cream prints and tan prints for blocks (collectively referred to as "light")

⅞ yard *total* of assorted red prints for blocks and sashing

¼ yard of red print for binding

1 yard of fabric for backing

24" × 36" piece of batting or flannel

## cutting

*All measurements include ¼"-wide seam allowances.*

**From the assorted light prints, cut a *total* of:**
+ 24 rectangles, 1½" × 3½"
+ 24 rectangles, 1½" × 2½"
+ 120 squares, 1½" × 1½"
+ 24 squares, 2" × 2"

**From the assorted red prints, cut a *total* of:**
+ 202 squares, 1½" × 1½"
+ 24 squares, 2" × 2"
+ 11 rectangles, 1½" × 9½"

**From the red print for binding, cut:**
+ 3 strips, 1½" × 42"

### SEEING RED

*Early red fabrics, known as Turkey reds, originated in the Middle East, including Turkey. Turkey red prints were clean and bright and sported blue, yellow, green, and white figures. Later in the nineteenth century, fabrics with a black print on a red background became popular and were known as Garibaldi red fabrics (named after Giuseppe Garibaldi, an Italian folk hero whose followers wore bright red shirts). Also popular during the late 1800s was burgundy with a white motif, called claret.*

PIECED AND
MACHINE
QUILTED BY
Annette Plog

♦♦♦

FINISHED QUILT
19½" × 31½"
FINISHED BLOCK
9" × 9"

# making the blocks

Use a ¼" seam allowance. Press all seam allowances as indicated by the arrows in the illustrations.

1 Draw a diagonal line from corner to corner on the wrong side of a light 2" square and layer it on top of a red 2" square, right sides together. Sew ¼" from both sides of the drawn line. Cut on the line to yield two half-square-triangle units. Trim the units to 1½" square, including seam allowances. Make 48 units.

Make 48 units,
1½" × 1½".

2 Arrange four red 1½" squares, three light 1½" squares, and one light 1½" × 2½" rectangle in three rows. Sew the pieces into rows; join the rows to make a unit that measures 3½" square, including seam allowances. Make four units.

Make 4 units,
3½" × 3½".

3 Arrange three red 1½" squares, two half-square-triangle units, one light 1½" square, and one light 1½" × 3½" rectangle in three rows. Sew the pieces into rows; join the rows to make a unit that measures 3½" square, including seam allowances. Make four units.

Make 4 units, 3½" × 3½".

4 Arrange five red and four light 1½" squares in three rows. Sew the pieces into rows; join the rows to make a unit that measures 3½" square, including seam allowances.

Make 1 unit, 3½" × 3½".

5 Arrange the units from steps 2–4 in three rows. Sew the units into rows; join the rows to make a block that measures 9½" square, including seam allowances. Repeat to make a total of six blocks.

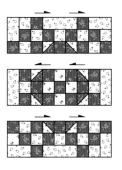 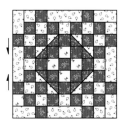

Make 6 blocks, 9½" × 9½".

# assembling the quilt top

1 Join two red 1½" × 9½" rectangles and one red 1½" square to make a sashing strip. Make four sashing strips that measure 1½" × 19½", including seam allowances.

Make 4 strips,
1½" × 19½".

2 Refer to the quilt assembly diagram below to arrange two blocks and one red 1½" × 9½" rectangle. Sew together to make a block row that measures 9½" × 19½", including seam allowances. Repeat to make a total of three block rows.

3 Join the block rows alternately with the sashing strips. Add a sashing strip to the top and the bottom of the quilt top. The completed quilt top should measure 19½" × 31½".

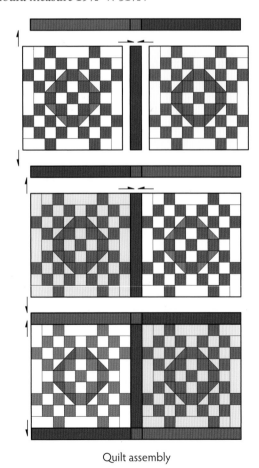

Quilt assembly

# finishing the quilt

For help with any of the following finishing steps, visit ShopMartingale.com/HowtoQuilt for free downloadable instructions.

1 Layer the table-topper top, batting or flannel, and backing. Baste the layers together.

2 Quilt by hand or machine. The topper shown is machine quilted using a diagonal crosshatch pattern.

3 Use the red 1½"-wide strips to make single-fold binding; attach the binding to the topper.

# Queen's Cross

*Antique quilts are a great place to find inspiration. Queen's Cross was inspired by a small, scrappy antique quilt. I love the cross in the center of these blocks and how the sashing allows the quilter to use lots of fun plaids and stripes. The color scheme gives this cutie an autumn feel, but use your creative license and make it your own.*

## materials

*Yardage is based on 42"-wide fabric.*

⅛ yard *each* of 6 assorted light prints for blocks

⅛ yard *each* of 6 assorted cheddar prints for blocks

⅛ yard *each* of 6 assorted gray prints for blocks

⅛ yard *each* of 6 assorted black prints for blocks

⅛ yard of light dot print for sashing

¼ yard of cheddar large-scale print for inner border

½ yard of black check for outer border and binding

⅞ yard of fabric for backing

28" × 34" piece of batting or flannel

## cutting

*All measurements include ¼"-wide seam allowances.*

**From *each* of the assorted light prints, cut:**
+ 4 squares, 2½" × 2½" (24 total)

**From *each* of the assorted cheddar prints, cut:**
+ 4 squares, 2½" × 2½" (24 total)

**From *each* of the assorted gray prints, cut:**
+ 8 rectangles, 1¼" × 2" (48 total)
+ 8 squares, 1¼" × 1¼" (48 total)

**From *each* of the assorted black prints, cut:**
+ 8 rectangles, 1¼" × 4¼" (48 total)
+ 3 squares, 1¼" × 1¼" (18 total)

**From the light dot print, cut:**
+ 17 rectangles, 1¼" × 5¾"

**From the cheddar large-scale print, cut:**
+ 2 strips, 1¼" × 23¾"
+ 2 strips, 1¼" × 19¼"

**From the black check, cut:**
+ 2 strips, 2½" × 25¼"
+ 2 strips, 2½" × 23¼"
+ 3 strips, 1½" × 42"

# making the blocks

Use a ¼" seam allowance. Press all seam allowances as indicated by the arrows in the illustrations.

1  Draw a diagonal line from corner to corner on the wrong side of a light 2½" square and layer it on top of a cheddar 2½" square, right sides together. Sew ¼" from both sides of the drawn line. Cut on the line to yield two half-square-triangle units. Trim the units to 2" square, including seam allowances. Make eight units from *each* of the cheddar/light combinations (48 total).

Make 48 units,
2" × 2".

2  Arrange four matching units from step 1, four matching gray 1¼" × 2" rectangles, and one black 1¼" square in three rows as shown. Sew the pieces into rows; join the rows to make a 4¼"-square center unit.

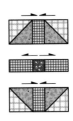 

Make 1 unit,
4¼" × 4¼".

3  Arrange the center unit, four matching black 1¼" × 4¼" rectangles, and four matching gray 1¼" squares in three rows as shown. Sew the pieces into rows; join the rows to make a 5¾"-square block. Repeat to make a total of 12 blocks.

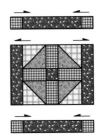 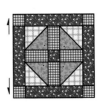

Make 12 blocks,
5¾" × 5¾".

## PRINTS TO DIE FOR

*Mourning prints were all the rage in the late 1800s. After the death of Prince Albert in 1861, Queen Victoria wore mourning clothing for the rest of her life. The fashion was copied in America, and soon dark fabrics were found in quilts too. The mourning fabrics were typically black, gray, purple, or indigo, with small white printed motifs.*

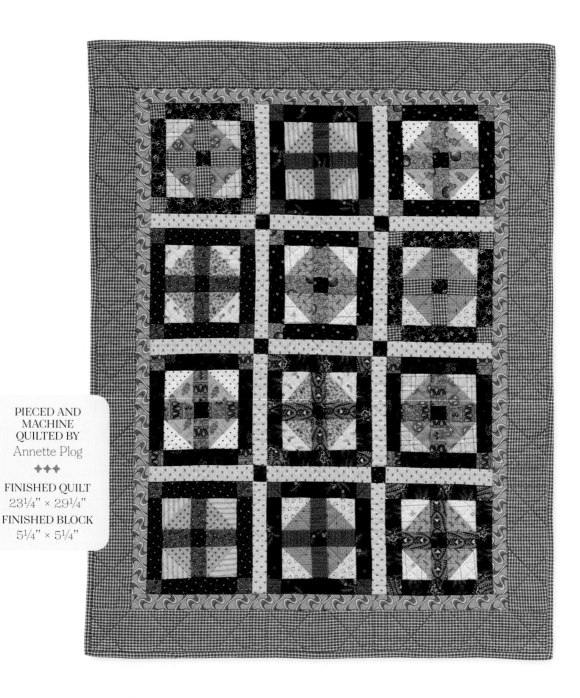

PIECED AND
MACHINE
QUILTED BY
Annette Plog
✦✦✦
FINISHED QUILT
23¼" × 29¼"
FINISHED BLOCK
5¼" × 5¼"

# assembling the quilt top

1 Refer to the quilt assembly diagram on page 25 to join three blocks and two light dot 1¼" × 5¾" rectangles. Repeat to make four block rows that measure 5¾" × 17¾", including seam allowances.

2 Arrange three light dot 1¼" × 5¾" rectangles and two black 1¼" squares to make a sashing row. Repeat to make three sashing rows that measure 1¼" × 17¾", including seam allowances.

3 Arrange the block rows and the sashing rows alternately. Sew the rows together. The quilt top should measure 17¾" × 23¾", including seam allowances.

4 Sew the cheddar 1¼" × 23¾" strips to opposite sides of the quilt top. Sew the cheddar 1¼" × 19¼" strips to the top and bottom of the quilt top. The top should measure 19¼" × 25¼", including seam allowances.

5 Sew the black check 2½" × 25¼" strips to opposite sides of the quilt top. Sew the black check 2½" × 23¼" strips to the top and bottom of the quilt top. The completed quilt top should measure 23¼" × 29¼".

## finishing the quilt

For help with any of the following finishing steps, visit ShopMartingale.com/HowtoQuilt for downloadable instructions.

1 Layer the quilt top, batting or flannel, and backing. Baste the layers together.

2 Quilt by hand or machine. The quilt shown is machine quilted using a diagonal crosshatch pattern.

3 Use the black 1½"-wide strips to make single-fold binding; attach the binding to the quilt.

## PIECING PLAIDS, CHECKS & STRIPES

*Queen's Cross, a Shoofly variation, is named in honor of Queen Victoria. I used a happy mix of plaids, stripes, and checks in the quilt. When these printed designs are used in your quilts, don't fuss over getting all the lines straight. Just do your best cutting and piecing and enjoy. Antique quilts aren't perfect, so learn to love your creation and don't sweat the small stuff!*

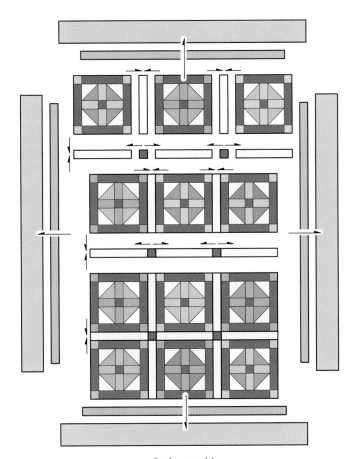

Quilt assembly

# Fly Away Home

*Fly Away Home was created with blocks acquired through a block exchange with several quilting friends. The small Birds in the Air blocks are only 3" square, and each block is unique, adding a lot of variety to the quilt. Exchanging blocks or scraps with fellow quilters is a great way to make a quilt scrappier than you could on your own.*

## materials

*Yardage is based on 42"-wide fabric.*

1 yard *total* of assorted cream prints for blocks

1⅝ yards *total* of assorted red, navy, brown, blue, rust, and madder prints for blocks (collectively referred to as "dark")

½ yard of tan floral for setting pieces and border

¼ yard of navy print for binding

1¼ yards of fabric for backing

39" × 43" piece of batting or flannel

## cutting

*All measurements include ¼"-wide seam allowances.*

**From the assorted cream prints, cut 49 *matching* sets of:**

+ 5 squares, 2" × 2" (245 total)

**From the assorted dark prints, cut 49 *matching* sets of:**

+ 5 squares, 2" × 2" (245 total)
+ 2 squares, 2½" × 2½" (98 total)

**From the tan floral, cut:**

+ 7 squares, 5½" × 5½"; cut into quarters diagonally to yield 28 side setting triangles (2 will be extra)
+ 2 squares, 3" × 3"; cut in half diagonally to yield 4 corner setting triangles
+ 4 strips, 1½" × 42"; crosscut into:
    2 strips, 1½" × 34½"
    2 strips, 1½" × 32¼"

**From the navy print, cut:**

+ 4 strips, 1½" × 42"

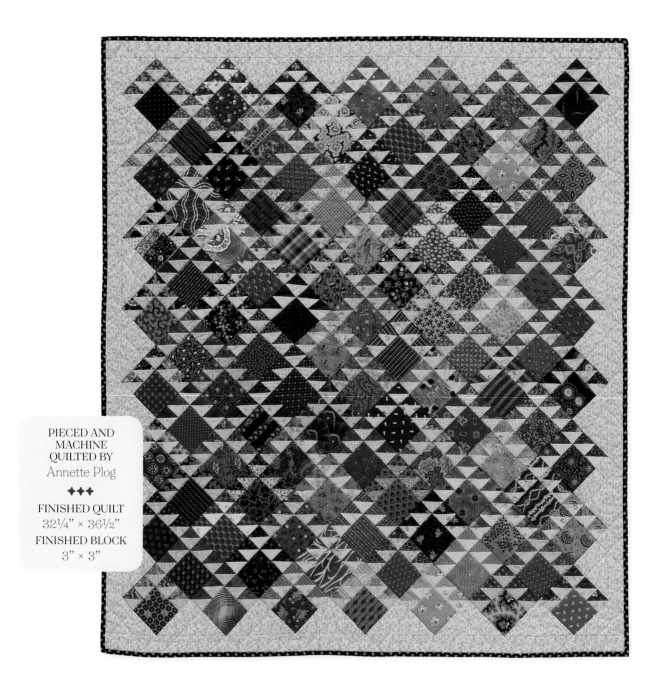

PIECED AND
MACHINE
QUILTED BY
Annette Plog
◆◆◆
FINISHED QUILT
32¼" × 36½"
FINISHED BLOCK
3" × 3"

# making the blocks

Use a ¼" seam allowance. Press all seam allowances as indicated by the arrows in the illustrations.

1 Arrange the light and dark 2" squares into 49 matching sets of five light and five dark squares. Draw a diagonal line from corner to corner on the wrong side of a light square and layer it on top of a dark square, right sides together. Sew ¼" from both sides of the drawn line. Cut on the line to yield two half-square-triangle units. Trim the units to 1½" square, including seam allowances. Repeat to make 49 sets of 10 matching half-square-triangle units (490 total).

Make 49 sets of
10 matching units,
1½" × 1½".

2 Arrange five matching units and one dark 2½" square (which can be matching or not; see "Mix It Up" at right) in two rows as shown. Sew the units in the top row together. Join the small units in the second row, and then add the joined units to the square. Join the rows. Use the clipping trick (page 30) where the seams come together. The block should measure 3½" square, including seam allowances. Repeat to make a total of 98 blocks.

Make 98 blocks,
3½" × 3½".

# assembling the quilt top

1 Refer to the quilt assembly diagram below to arrange the blocks, side setting triangles, and corner setting triangles in diagonal rows.

2 Sew the blocks and side setting triangles together into rows. Join the rows and add the corner triangles last. The quilt top should measure 31¼" × 34½", including seam allowances.

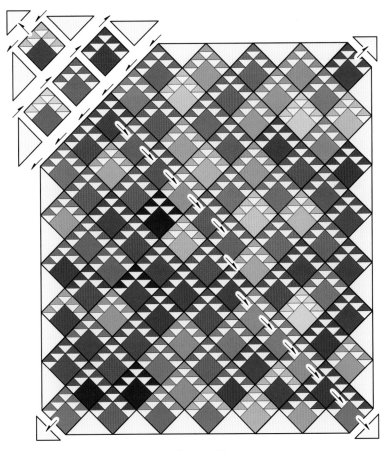

Quilt assembly

3 Sew the tan floral 1½" × 34½" strips to opposite sides of the quilt top. Sew the tan floral 1½" × 32¼" strips to the top and bottom. The quilt top should measure 32¼" × 36½".

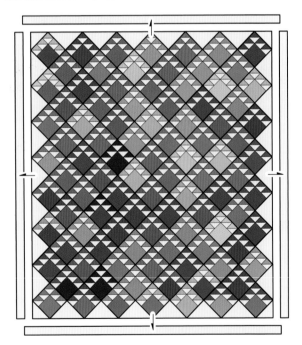

Adding the border

## finishing the quilt

For help with any of the following finishing steps, visit ShopMartingale.com/HowtoQuilt for downloadable instructions.

1 Layer the quilt top, batting or flannel, and backing. Baste the layers together.

2 Quilt by hand or machine. The quilt shown is machine quilted using a diagonal grid pattern.

3 Use the navy 1½"-wide strips to make single-fold binding; attach the binding to the quilt.

### CLIPPING TRICK

*To maintain crisp block points, reduce bulk in a seam, and allow blocks to nest together, try this clipping trick in places where seams intersect.*

*Clip the seam allowances ¼" from each side of the seam intersections. Then press the seam allowances away from the half-square-triangle units. This is an easy way to help your blocks lie flat and look great.*

# Attic Stairs

*Attic Stairs features a variation of the Jacob's Ladder block. The "ladder" is shorter than in the traditional block, resembling the short steps that lead to an attic. I love the sashing of Lancaster blue—a clear, pretty blue that plays well with the browns, teals, and golds in the blocks.*

## materials

*Yardage is based on 42"-wide fabric.*

¼ yard *each* of 18 prints for blocks: 6 light prints, 6 medium brown prints, and 6 dark brown prints

¼ yard *each* of 6 prints for block sashing: 2 medium brown prints, 3 blue prints, and 1 gold print

2⅞ yards of Lancaster blue print for sashing, border, and binding

4⅔ yards of fabric for backing

65" × 83" piece of batting

## cutting

*All measurements include ¼"-wide seam allowances.*

**From *each* of the light prints, cut:**
+ 16 squares, 3" × 3" (96 total)

**From *each* of the medium brown prints, cut:**
+ 16 squares, 3" × 3" (96 total)

**From *each* of the dark brown prints, cut:**
+ 42 squares, 2½" × 2½" (252 total)

**From *each* of the medium brown, blue, and gold prints for block sashing, cut:**
+ 8 rectangles, 2½" × 6½" (48 total)
+ 4 squares, 2" × 2" (24 total)
+ 4 rectangles, 1½" × 2" (24 total)
+ 1 square, 1½" × 1½" (6 total)

**From the blue print, cut:**
+ 16 strips, 4½" × 42"; crosscut 9 *of the strips* into 17 rectangles, 4½" × 14½"
+ 8 strips, 2½" × 42"

## making the blocks

Use a ¼" seam allowance. Press all seam allowances as indicated by the arrows in the illustrations.

1 Choose the following pieces for one block: eight matching light 3" squares, eight matching medium brown 3" squares, 21 matching dark brown 2½" squares, and four matching medium brown, blue, or gold 2½" × 6½" rectangles. Draw a diagonal line from corner to corner on the wrong side of a light square and layer it on top of a medium brown square, right sides together. Sew ¼" from both sides of the drawn line. Cut on the line to yield two half-square-triangle units. Trim the units to 2½" square, including seam allowances. Make 16 units.

Make 16 units, 2½" × 2½".

2 Lay out four half-square-triangle units and five dark brown squares in three rows. Sew the pieces together in rows, and then join the rows to make one ladder unit that measures 6½" square, including seam allowances. Make four.

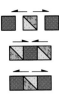

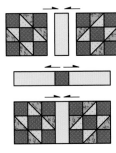

Make 4 ladder units,
6½" × 6½".

3 Arrange the four ladder units, the four rectangles, and the remaining dark brown square in three rows. Sew the pieces together in rows, and then join the rows. The block should measure 14½" square, including seam allowances. Make 12 blocks.

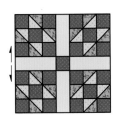

Make 12 blocks,
14½" × 14½".

## BLUE TIMES TWO

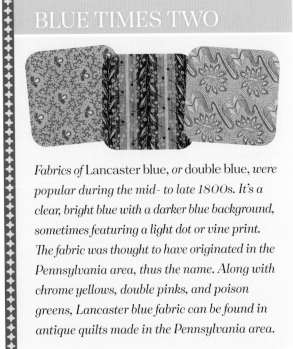

*Fabrics of Lancaster blue, or double blue, were popular during the mid- to late 1800s. It's a clear, bright blue with a darker blue background, sometimes featuring a light dot or vine print. The fabric was thought to have originated in the Pennsylvania area, thus the name. Along with chrome yellows, double pinks, and poison greens, Lancaster blue fabric can be found in antique quilts made in the Pennsylvania area.*

# assembling the quilt top

1 From the medium brown, blue, and gold prints, choose four matching 2" squares, four matching 1½" × 2" rectangles, and one 1½" square. Arrange the pieces in three rows. Sew the pieces together in rows, and then join the rows to make a cornerstone unit that measures 4½" square, including seam allowances. Repeat to make six units.

Make 6 units,
4½" × 4½".

PIECED BY
Annette Plog
MACHINE
QUILTED BY
Sheri Mecom
♦♦♦
FINISHED QUILT
58½" × 76½"
FINISHED BLOCK
14" × 14"

2 Refer to the quilt assembly diagram on page 35 to sew three blocks and two blue 4½" × 14½" rectangles together. Make four block rows that measure 14½" × 50½", including seam allowances.

3 Sew three blue 4½" × 14½" rectangles and two cornerstone units together to make a sashing row. Make three sashing rows that measure 4½" × 50½", including seam allowances.

4 Sew the block and sashing rows together. The quilt top should measure 50½" × 68½", including seam allowances.

**5** Sew together the blue 4½" × 42" strips to make one long strip. From this strip, cut two strips, 4½" × 68½", and sew them to opposite sides of the quilt top. Cut two strips, 4½" × 58½", and sew them to the top and bottom of the quilt top. The quilt top should measure 58½" × 76½".

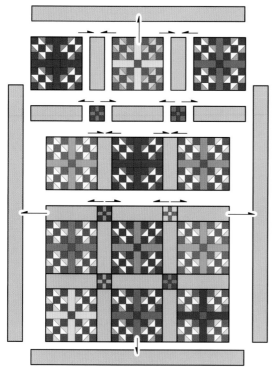

Quilt assembly

# finishing the quilt

For help with any of the following finishing steps, visit ShopMartingale.com/HowtoQuilt for downloadable instructions.

**1** Layer the quilt top, batting, and backing. Baste the layers together.

**2** Quilt by hand or machine. The quilt shown is machine quilted using an allover swirl pattern.

**3** Use the blue 2½"-wide strips to make the binding; attach the binding to the quilt.

## GO FOR THE GOLD

*The unexpected pop of gold fabric, used as sashing in some of the blocks, adds spark and catches the eye. Don't shy away from adding a "surprise" fabric to your quilts. These unusual choices add joy to your creations.*

# Calico Baskets

*Who could resist these sweet little baskets? I'm able to enjoy them thanks to my friend Marilyn, who put together the block exchange for this quilt. To make the handles, try back-basting appliqué. If you're not familiar with this technique, give it a try; you'll find that it yields admirably accurate results. It's much easier than you'd think, and the baskets are small, meaning this is a great time to learn a new technique.*

## materials

*Yardage is based on 42"-wide fabric. Fat eighths measure 9" × 21".*

24 fat eighths of assorted medium and dark small-scale prints for blocks

1 yard of cream small-scale print for blocks

1⅛ yards of tan stripe for setting squares

½ yard of brown print for binding

2½ yards of fabric for backing

43" × 59" piece of batting or flannel

Template plastic

### MIXED-UP BASKETS

*Some of the blocks have basket handles that match the three triangles across the top of the basket, and some have handles that match the two squares in the middle. Dark and light values are also used in different positions in the blocks. There are many ways to arrange the colors and values in these blocks. While cutting the pieces for a block, you can mix up the triangles and squares for your own scrappy baskets.*

## cutting

*All measurements include ¼"-wide seam allowances. Cutting fabric for 1 basket at a time makes planning easier and helps keep your fabrics organized.*

### CUTTING FOR 1 BASKET (Cut 59 total.)

**From 1 print, cut:**
+ 2 squares, 1⅞" × 1⅞"; cut in half diagonally to yield 4 small triangles (3 will be used per basket; set 1 aside for a scrappy basket or discard)
+ 1 square, 1½" × 1½"

**From a different print, cut:**
+ 1 square, 1⅞" × 1⅞"; cut in half diagonally to yield 2 small triangles
+ 2 squares, 1½" × 1½"
+ 1 square, 3" × 3"; cut in half diagonally to yield 2 large triangles (1 will be used for basket handle; set 1 aside for another basket)

*(Continued on page 38)*

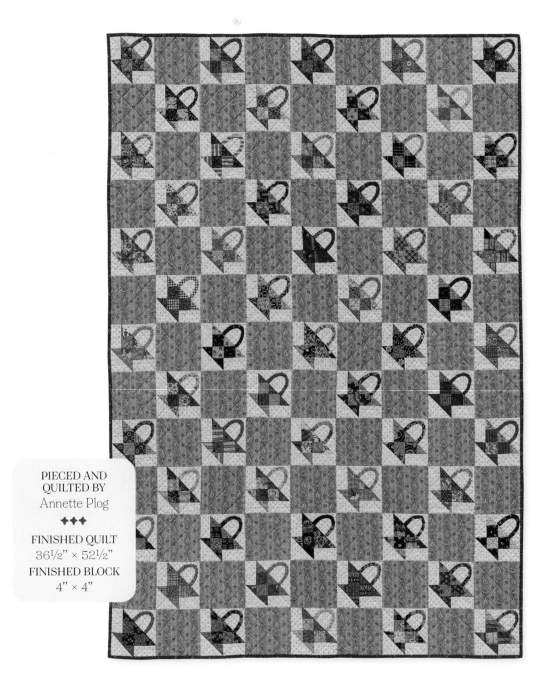

PIECED AND
QUILTED BY
Annette Plog

✦✦✦

FINISHED QUILT
36½" × 52½"
FINISHED BLOCK
4" × 4"

*(Continued from page 36)*

## CUTTING FOR BLOCK BACKGROUNDS, SETTING SQUARES, AND BINDING

**From the tan stripe, cut:**

✦ 8 strips, 4½" × 42"; crosscut into 58 squares, 4½" × 4½"

**From the brown print, cut:**

✦ 5 strips, 2½" × 42"

**From the cream print, cut:**

✦ 3 strips, 4" × 42"; crosscut into 30 squares, 4" × 4". Cut the squares in half diagonally to yield 60 large triangles (1 will be extra; cut oversized for trimming later).

✦ 8 strips, 1½" × 42"; crosscut into 118 rectangles, 1½" × 2½"

✦ 3 strips, 2⅞" × 42"; crosscut into 30 squares, 2⅞" × 2⅞". Cut the squares in half diagonally to yield 60 small triangles (1 will be extra).

## PIECING WITH STRIPES

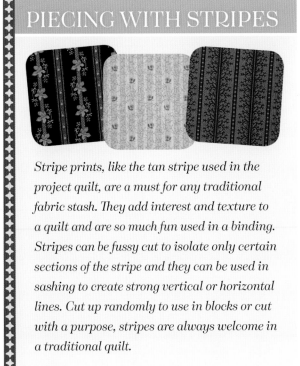

*Stripe prints, like the tan stripe used in the project quilt, are a must for any traditional fabric stash. They add interest and texture to a quilt and are so much fun used in a binding. Stripes can be fussy cut to isolate only certain sections of the stripe and they can be used in sashing to create strong vertical or horizontal lines. Cut up randomly to use in blocks or cut with a purpose, stripes are always welcome in a traditional quilt.*

## making the blocks

Use a ¼" seam allowance. Press all seam allowances as indicated by the arrows in the illustrations.

1 Arrange the print pieces for one block with two cream rectangles and one small cream triangle. Sew the pieces into rows; then join the rows to make a basket-base unit. Make 59.

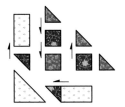 

Make 59 basket-base units.

## TRY BACK-BASTING APPLIQUÉ

*Back basting is a fun and accurate way to hand appliqué—all you need to do is follow the basting line when you appliqué the handle (see page 40). And if you baste several little basket handles to their background triangles, they become a small, portable hand-appliqué project. Once the basket handles are finished, you can complete the Basket blocks. Easy!*

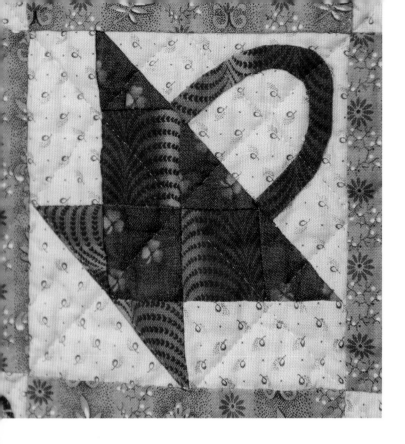

2 Using the pattern on page 41, make a plastic template. Use the template to trace the basket handle onto the wrong side of a large cream triangle, centering the handle on the triangle. Place the cream triangle, right side down, on the wrong side of the dark triangle you cut for the basket's handle. Baste the fabrics together along the drawn handle line.

Basting the handle

3 Cut the dark fabric away, leaving a seam allowance that's slightly wider than ⅛".

Trimming the handle

4 At the base of the handle, slip a threaded sewing needle under the basting thread and remove two

to three stitches. From the wrong side of the handle fabric, insert the needle into the first basting perforation. Using your needle to turn under the seam allowance along the basting line, stitch both curved edges of the handle to the background, removing a few basting stitches at a time as you work your way along. Repeat to make a total of 59 basket handles.

 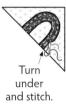 

Unpick basting stitches.  Turn under and stitch.  Make 59 basket handles.

5 Sew together the basket-base unit and the basket handle, pressing as shown. Trim the block to measure 4½" square, including seam allowances. Repeat to make 59 Basket blocks.

Make 59 Basket blocks, 4½" × 4½".

## assembling the quilt top

1 Refer to the quilt assembly diagram below to arrange the blocks and tan stripe squares alternately in 13 rows of nine pieces each.

2 Sew the blocks and setting squares together into rows. Join the rows. The quilt top should measure 36½" × 52½".

## finishing the quilt

For help with any of the following finishing steps, visit ShopMartingale.com for downloadable instructions.

1 Layer the quilt top, batting or flannel, and backing. Baste the layers together.

2 Quilt by hand or machine. The quilt shown is machine quilted using a grid pattern.

3 Use the brown 2½"-wide strips to make the binding; attach the binding to the quilt.

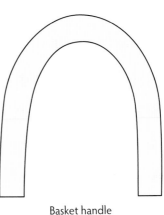

Basket handle

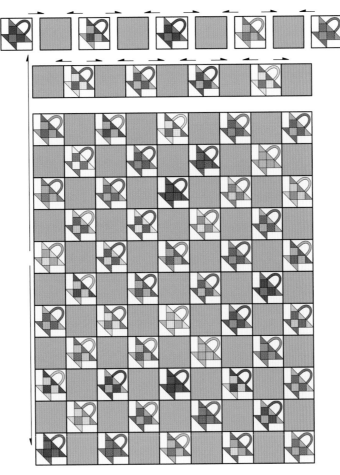

Quilt assembly

# Chintz Nine Patch

*The simplicity of an Uneven Nine Patch block allows your fabric choices to be the star of the quilt. The blocks are a wonderful way to showcase large florals, pretty chintz fabrics, and ombré stripes. Need more chintz prints? Get a block exchange group together and share fabrics. Let the beautiful fabrics stand out and shine.*

## materials

*Yardage is based on 42"-wide fabric.*

2 yards *total* of assorted large-scale and small-scale chintz prints for blocks

1⅔ yards of cream solid for blocks

3 yards of large-scale floral for setting squares and binding

4⅞ yards of fabric for backing

75" × 87" piece of batting

## cutting

*All measurements include ¼"-wide seam allowances. Cutting fabric for 1 block at a time makes planning easier and helps keep your fabrics organized.*

### CUTTING FOR 1 BLOCK (Cut 72 total.)

**From 1 chintz print, cut:**
+ 4 squares, 2" × 2"
+ 1 square, 3½" × 3½"

### CUTTING FOR BLOCK BACKGROUNDS, SETTING SQUARES, AND BINDING

**From the cream solid, cut:**
+ 288 rectangles, 2" × 3½"

**From the large-scale floral, cut:**
+ 71 squares, 6½" × 6½"
+ 8 strips, 2½" × 42"

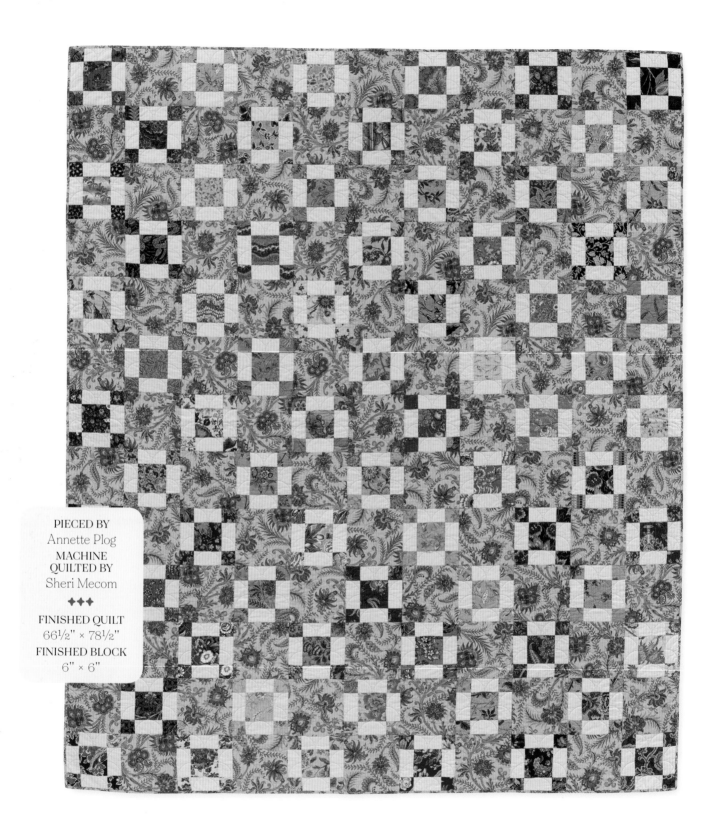

PIECED BY
Annette Plog
MACHINE
QUILTED BY
Sheri Mecom

✦✦✦

FINISHED QUILT
66½" × 78½"
FINISHED BLOCK
6" × 6"

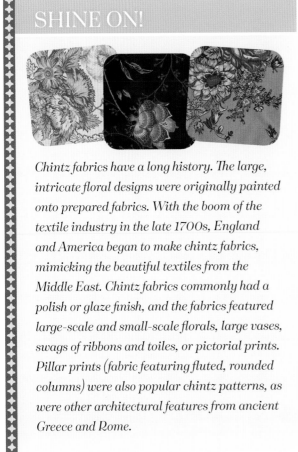

Chintz fabrics have a long history. The large, intricate floral designs were originally painted onto prepared fabrics. With the boom of the textile industry in the late 1700s, England and America began to make chintz fabrics, mimicking the beautiful textiles from the Middle East. Chintz fabrics commonly had a polish or glaze finish, and the fabrics featured large-scale and small-scale florals, large vases, swags of ribbons and toiles, or pictorial prints. Pillar prints (fabric featuring fluted, rounded columns) were also popular chintz patterns, as were other architectural features from ancient Greece and Rome.

## making the blocks

Use a ¼" seam allowance. Press all seam allowances as indicated by the arrows in the illustrations.

Arrange four chintz 2" squares, one chintz 3½" square, and four cream 2" × 3½" rectangles in three rows. Sew the pieces into rows; join the rows to make a block that measures 6½" square, including seam allowances. Make 72 blocks.

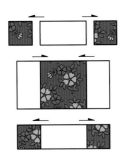

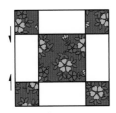

Make 72 blocks,
6½" × 6½".

## assembling the quilt top

Refer to the quilt assembly diagram below to arrange the blocks and floral 6½" squares alternately into 13 rows of 11 pieces each. Sew the pieces together in rows, and then sew the rows together. The quilt top should measure 66½" × 78½".

## finishing the quilt

For help with any of the following finishing steps, visit ShopMartingale.com/HowtoQuilt for downloadable instructions.

1 Layer the quilt top, batting, and backing. Baste the layers together.

2 Quilt by hand or machine. The quilt shown is machine quilted using a clamshell pattern.

3 Use the floral 2½"-wide strips to make the binding; attach the binding to the quilt.

### CHOOSE A REPRODUCTION QUILTING DESIGN

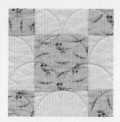

*If you're reproducing an antique quilt and carefully choosing the quilt's fabrics, using a quilting design that's true to the time period is equally as important. Chintz Nine Patch is a reproduction of an early 1800s quilt, so the machine quilter, Sheri Mecom, suggested an overall clamshell pattern, which was often used in quilts of the time period.*

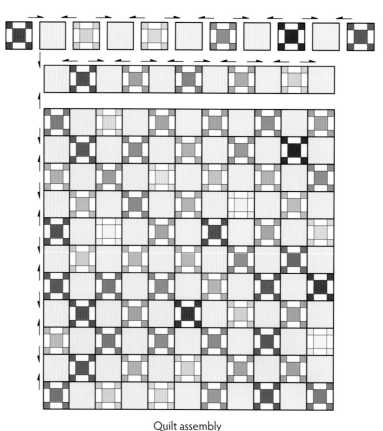

Quilt assembly

# T for Two

Brown quilts have always been a favorite of mine; from light neutral to warm chocolate, brown has a lot of variety. A one-color quilt can be understated but stunning in its appeal. The Double T block has a history that dates to the early 1800s, but took on a new cause during the temperance movement in the latter part of that century. Women and their quilts were always on the cutting edge of current events!

## materials

*Yardage is based on 42"-wide fabric.*

4 yards *total* of assorted cream prints for blocks

4¼ yards *total* of brown, rust, and madder prints for blocks (collectively referred to as "dark")

4⅜ yards of brown print for setting pieces and binding

7⅛ yards of fabric for backing

85" × 98" piece of batting

### BLOCK VARIETY

*Choose one light and one dark fabric for each block or choose a variety of fabrics for a scrappy look. Notice some of the blocks use two different darks for the T shapes. One block has three Ts from one dark fabric and one from another dark. It all adds to the uniqueness of the quilt.*

## cutting

*All measurements include ¼"-wide seam allowances. Cutting fabric for 1 block at a time makes planning easier and helps keep your fabrics organized.*

### CUTTING FOR 1 BLOCK (Cut 42 total.)

**From 1 cream print, cut:**
+ 2 squares, 4" × 4"
+ 2 squares, 2½" × 2½"
+ 8 rectangles, 2" × 3½"

**From 1 dark print, cut:**
+ 2 squares, 4" × 4"
+ 2 squares, 2½" × 2½"
+ 16 squares, 2" × 2"

### CUTTING FOR SETTING PIECES AND BINDING

**From the brown print, cut:**
+ 30 squares, 9½" × 9½"
+ 6 squares, 14" × 14"; cut into quarters diagonally to yield 24 side setting triangles (2 will be extra)
+ 2 squares, 7¼" × 7¼"; cut in half diagonally to yield 4 corner setting triangles
+ 9 strips, 2½" × 42"

## NATURAL NEUTRALS

*Brown fabrics are the new neutral of the quilting world. Brown doesn't compete with other colors but complements them. Many brown fabrics were originally made with natural madder dye, which produced a coppery tone. Colors produced with madder included a warm dark brown, light tans, medium browns, and orangey browns, along with brick red, salmon pink, and lavender grays. Dark brown and chocolate browns were also popular fabrics during the 1800s.*

# making the blocks

Use a ¼" seam allowance. Press all seam allowances as indicated by the arrows in the illustrations.

1 Choose the pieces for one block. Draw a diagonal line from corner to corner on the wrong side of a light 4" square and layer it on top of a dark 4" square, right sides together. Sew ¼" from both sides of the drawn line. Cut on the line to yield two half-square-triangle units. Trim each unit to 3½" square, including seam allowances. Repeat to make four units.

Make 4 units,
3½" × 3½".

2 Repeat step 1 with a light and a dark 2½" square. Trim the units to 2" square, including seam allowances. Make four units.

Make 4 units,
2" × 2".

3 Draw a diagonal line from corner to corner on the wrong side of the dark 2" squares. Place a dark square on one end of a cream 2" × 3½" rectangle, right sides together. Sew on the drawn line. Trim ¼" beyond the sewn line and flip the corner up. Repeat on the other end to make a flying-geese unit that measures 2" × 3½", including seam allowances. Make eight flying-geese units.

Make 8 units,
2" × 3½".

4 Arrange the 3½" half-square-triangle units, flying-geese units, and 2" half-square-triangle units in three rows as shown. Sew the pieces into rows; join the rows to make a block. The block should measure 9½" square, including seam allowances. Repeat to make 42 blocks.

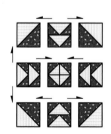

Make 42 blocks,
9½" × 9½".

PIECED BY
Annette Plog
MACHINE
QUILTED BY
Sheri Mecom
◆◆◆
FINISHED QUILT
77" × 89¾"
FINISHED BLOCK
9" × 9"

## assembling the quilt top

Refer to the quilt assembly diagram to arrange the blocks and the brown setting triangles and squares in diagonal rows. Sew the blocks, squares, and side triangles together into rows. Join the rows and add the corner triangles last. The quilt top should measure 77" × 89¾".

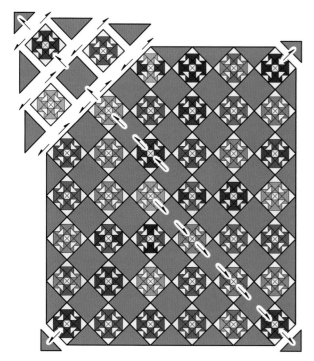

Quilt assembly

## finishing the quilt

For help with any of the following finishing steps, visit ShopMartingale.com/HowtoQuilt for downloadable instructions.

1. Layer the quilt top, batting, and backing. Baste the layers together.

2. Quilt by hand or machine. The quilt shown is machine quilted using an allover feather pattern.

3. Use the brown 2½"-wide strips to make the binding; attach the binding to the quilt.

### BLOCK ERRORS? NO PROBLEM!

*Whether you accidentally make a block that is pieced incorrectly or one that uses the wrong fabric, you can still use it in your quilt. As long as the block is the correct size, it can be slipped into your quilt without taking away from the overall design. Many antique quilts contain piecing mistakes or mismatched pieces. So include these blocks and challenge others to find the "wrong" block!*

# Prussian Blue Stars

*Gorgeous block alert—half-square triangles pieced together make sparkling diamonds. Stars are a traditional quilt pattern, but elongating the star points creates a unique design. The featured fabrics are Prussian blues and the background fabric is a blue toile, giving this quilt a soft and tranquil feel.*

## materials

*Yardage is based on 42"-wide fabric. Fat eighths measure 9" × 21".*

8 fat eighths of assorted Prussian blue prints for blocks
1⅛ yards of light blue toile for blocks
⅓ yard of blue stripe for sashing
1 yard of Prussian blue print for border and binding
2¾ yards of fabric for backing
49" × 49" piece of batting

### INDIGO ALTERNATIVE

*Indigo-dyed fabrics were hard to come by and therefore expensive during the early part of the nineteenth century. Prussian blue, a cool, greenish-blue pigment created from minerals, was a low-cost alternative that appeared frequently in quilts made in the United States between 1830 and the mid-1850s. Prussian blue is seen commonly in chintz fabrics or printed with a light tan motif. Other names for this fabric were Berlin blue and Paris blue.*

## cutting

*All measurements include ¼"-wide seam allowances.*

### From *each* of the assorted Prussian blue fat eighths, cut:

✦ 2 strips, 3" × 21"; crosscut into 9 squares, 3" × 3" (72 total)

### From the light blue toile, cut:

✦ 6 strips, 3" × 42"; crosscut into 72 squares, 3" × 3"
✦ 6 strips, 2½" × 42"; crosscut into:
    9 squares, 2½" × 2½"
    36 rectangles, 2½" × 4½"

### From the blue stripe, cut:

✦ 4 strips, 2½" × 42"; crosscut into:
    2 strips, 2½" × 34½"
    6 rectangles, 2½" × 10½"

### From the Prussian blue print, cut:

✦ 5 strips, 4½" × 42"; crosscut 2 of the strips into
    2 strips, 4½" × 34½"
✦ 5 strips, 1½" × 42"

PIECED AND
MACHINE
QUILTED BY
Annette Plog

◆◆◆

FINISHED QUILT
42½" × 42½"
FINISHED BLOCK
10" × 10"

## making the blocks

Use a ¼" seam allowance. Press all seam allowances as indicated by the arrows in the illustrations.

1 Draw a diagonal line from corner to corner on the wrong side of a toile 3" square and layer it on top of a blue 3" square, right sides together. Sew ¼" from both sides of the drawn line. Cut on the line to yield two half-square-triangle units. Trim the units to 2½" square, including seam allowances. Make 16 units from *each* of the blue/toile combinations (144 total).

Make 9 sets of
16 matching units,
2½" × 2½".

2. Lay out 16 matching half-square-triangle units, four toile 2½" × 4½" rectangles, and one toile 2½" square in three rows. Sew the pieces into rows, and then sew the rows together to complete the block. The block should measure 10½" square, including seam allowances. Repeat to make nine blocks.

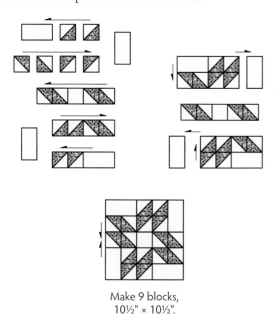

Make 9 blocks,
10½" × 10½".

## assembling the quilt top

1. Refer to the quilt assembly diagram on page 56 to sew together three blocks and two blue stripe 2½" × 10½" rectangles. Repeat to make three block rows that measure 10½" × 34½", including seam allowances.

2. Join the block rows and the two 2½" × 34½" blue stripe strips. The quilt top should measure 34½" square, including seam allowances.

3 Sew the Prussian blue 4½" × 34½" strips to opposite sides of the quilt center. Sew the three blue 4½" × 42" strips together end to end to make one long strip. From this strip cut two strips, 4½" × 42½", and sew these to the top and bottom of the quilt center. The quilt top should measure 42½" square.

## finishing the quilt

For help with any of the following finishing steps, visit ShopMartingale.com/HowtoQuilt for downloadable instructions.

1 Layer the quilt top, batting, and backing. Baste the layers together.

2 Quilt by hand or machine. The quilt shown is machine quilted using a diagonal crosshatch pattern.

3 Use the Prussian blue 1½"-wide strips to make single-fold binding; attach the binding to the quilt.

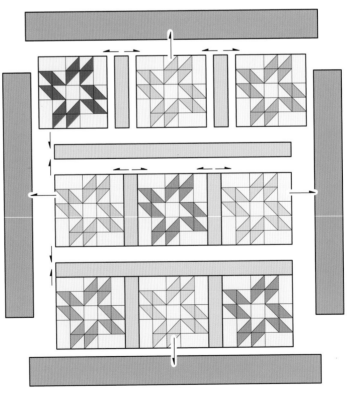

Quilt assembly

# Hopscotch

*Happy-go-lucky blocks hopscotch their way across a field of dusty purple, creating a quilt that's bright and scrappy and simple to sew. Dig into your stash to make the Four Patch blocks as scrappy as you want, and choose a pretty purple for the sashing—it will tie everything together.*

## materials

*Yardage is based on 42"-wide fabric.*

2 strips, 1½" × 42" *each*, of 20 assorted light, medium, and dark prints for blocks (40 total)

1⅔ yards of cream solid for blocks

3 yards of purple print for sashing, border, and binding

4⅓ yards of fabric for backing

64" × 80" piece of batting

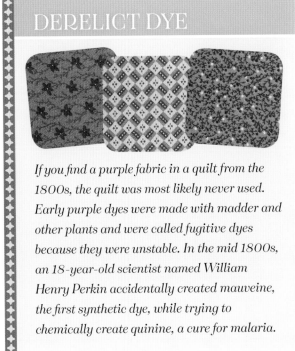

### DERELICT DYE

*If you find a purple fabric in a quilt from the 1800s, the quilt was most likely never used. Early purple dyes were made with madder and other plants and were called fugitive dyes because they were unstable. In the mid 1800s, an 18-year-old scientist named William Henry Perkin accidentally created mauveine, the first synthetic dye, while trying to chemically create quinine, a cure for malaria.*

## cutting

*All measurements include ¼"-wide seam allowances.*

**From the cream solid, cut:**
+ 6 strips, 2½" × 42"; crosscut into 82 squares, 2½" × 2½"
+ 6 strips, 4⅛" × 42"; crosscut into 48 squares, 4⅛" × 4⅛". Cut the squares into quarters diagonally to yield 192 triangles (A).
+ 3 strips, 2⅜" × 42"; crosscut into 41 squares, 2⅜" × 2⅜". Cut the squares in half diagonally to yield 82 triangles (B).
+ 2 strips, 1½" × 42"; crosscut into 28 rectangles, 1½" × 2½"
+ 1 strip, 2¾" × 42"; crosscut into 7 squares, 2¾" × 2¾". Cut the squares into quarters diagonally to yield 28 triangles (C).

**From the purple print, cut:**
+ 1 strip, 5½" × 42"; crosscut into 3 squares, 5½" × 5½". Cut the squares into quarters diagonally to yield 12 triangles (2 will be extra).
+ 21 strips, 3½" × 42"; crosscut 14 of the strips into:
    48 rectangles, 3½" × 9"
    18 squares, 3½" × 3½"
    2 squares, 3" × 3"; cut in half diagonally to
        yield 4 corner triangles
+ 7 strips, 2½" × 42"

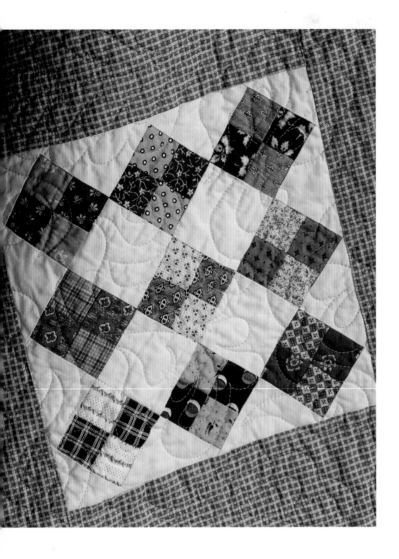

2 Sew together two matching segments to make a four-patch unit. Make 195 units that measure 2½" square, including seam allowances.

Make 195
four-patch units,
2½" × 2½".

3 Arrange nine four-patch units, four cream 2½" squares, eight cream A triangles, and four cream B triangles. Sew together in rows. Sew the rows together, adding the B triangles last, to make a Double Four Patch block. The block should measure 9" square, including seam allowances. Make 17 blocks.

Make 17 Double
Four Patch blocks,
9" × 9".

## making the blocks

Use a ¼" seam allowance. Press all seam allowances as indicated by the arrows in the illustrations.

1 Sew together two contrasting print 1½" × 42" strips to make a strip set. Repeat to make a total of 20 strip sets. Crosscut each strip set into 22 segments, 1½" wide, for a total of 440 segments that measure 1½" × 2½", including seam allowances (eight segments will be extra).

4 Arrange three four-patch units, three segments from step 1, one cream 2½" square, two cream 1½" × 2½" rectangles, four cream A triangles, one cream B triangle, and two cream C triangles. Sew together in rows. Sew the rows together, adding the B triangle last, to make a pieced setting triangle. Make 14.

Make 14 pieced
setting triangles.

1½"

Make 20 strip sets, 2½" × 42".
Cut 440 segments, 1½" × 2½".

PIECED BY
Annette Plog
MACHINE
QUILTED BY
Sheri Mecom
✦✦✦
FINISHED QUILT
55½" × 71¾"
FINISHED BLOCK
8½" × 8½"

## assembling the quilt top

1   Refer to the quilt assembly diagram to arrange the blocks, pieced setting triangles, purple 3½" × 9" rectangles, purple 3½" squares, and purple triangles in diagonal rows. Sew the pieces together in rows. Sew the rows together, adding the smaller purple corner triangles last. The quilt top should measure 49½" × 65¾", including seam allowances.

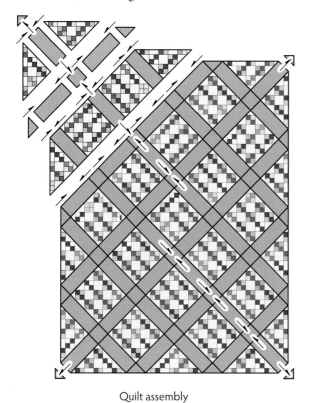

Quilt assembly

2   Sew the purple 3½" × 42" strips end to end to make one long strip. Cut two strips, 3½" × 65¾", and sew them to opposite sides of the quilt top. Cut two strips, 3½" × 55½", and sew them to the top and bottom of the quilt top. The quilt top should measure 55½" × 71¾".

## finishing the quilt

For help with any of the following finishing steps, visit ShopMartingale.com/HowtoQuilt for downloadable instructions.

1   Layer the quilt top, batting, and backing. Baste the layers together.

2   Quilt by hand or machine. The quilt shown is machine quilted using an allover swirl pattern.

3   Use the purple 2½"-wide strips to make the binding; attach the binding to the quilt.

# Fox-Trot

*The Fox and Geese block is traditional, but the zigzag sashing is not your average setting. I acquired the blocks through a monthly lunchtime block exchange organized by my friend Carol. The double pink sashing commands attention but doesn't overpower the scrappy blocks. Instead, it keeps your eye fox-trotting around the quilt.*

## materials

*Yardage is based on 42"-wide fabric.*

3 yards *total* of assorted shirtings and light prints for blocks and inner border (collectively referred to as "light")

2¼ yards *total* of brown, madder, tan, and red prints for blocks and inner border (collectively referred to as "dark")

4⅛ yards of double pink print for setting and corner triangles, outer border, and binding

5 yards of fabric for backing

79" × 88" piece of batting

## cutting

*All measurements include ¼"-wide seam allowances. Cutting fabric for 1 block or half block at a time makes planning easier and helps keep your fabrics organized.*

### CUTTING FOR 1 BLOCK (Cut 53 total.)

**From 1 light print, cut:**

+ 3 squares, 2½" × 2½"
+ 2 squares, 2⅜" × 2⅜"; cut in half diagonally to yield 4 triangles
+ 4 squares, 2" × 2"

**From 1 dark print, cut:**

+ 3 squares, 2½" × 2½"
+ 1 square, 3⅞" × 3⅞"; cut in half diagonally to yield 2 triangles

### CUTTING FOR 1 HALF BLOCK (Cut 6 total.)

**From 1 light print, cut:**

+ 2 squares, 2½" × 2½"
+ 3 squares, 2⅜" × 2⅜"; cut in half diagonally to yield 6 triangles

**From 1 dark print, cut:**

+ 2 squares, 2½" × 2½"
+ 1 square, 3⅞" × 3⅞"; cut in half diagonally to yield 2 triangles (1 will be extra)

### CUTTING FOR SETTING TRIANGLES, BORDERS, AND BINDING

**From the assorted light prints, cut a *total* of:**

+ 85 squares, 2½" × 2½"

**From the assorted dark prints, cut a *total* of:**

+ 85 squares, 2½" × 2½"

**From the double pink print, cut:**

+ 7 strips, 9¾" × 42"; crosscut into 26 squares, 9¾" × 9¾". Cut the squares into quarters diagonally to yield 104 triangles.
+ 2 strips, 5⅛" × 42"; crosscut into 8 squares, 5⅛" × 5⅛". Cut the squares in half diagonally to yield 16 triangles.
+ 8 strips, 4½" × 42"
+ 8 strips, 2½" × 42"

**PIECED BY**
Annette Plog
**MACHINE QUILTED BY**
Sheri Mecom
✦✦✦
**FINISHED QUILT**
71" × 79½"
**FINISHED BLOCK**
6" × 6"

## making the blocks

Use a ¼" seam allowance. Press all seam allowances as indicated by the arrows in the illustrations.

1 Choose the pieces for one block. Draw a diagonal line from corner to corner on the wrong side of a light 2½" square and layer it on top of a dark 2½" square, right sides together. Sew ¼" from both sides of the drawn line. Cut on the line to yield two half-square-triangle units. Trim the units to 2" square, including seam allowances. Make six units.

Make 6 units,
2" × 2".

# PINK PERFECTION

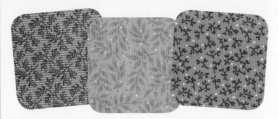

*Double pinks have been a perennial favorite of quilters for many years, frequently appearing in antique quilts. Often called* cinnamon pink *because of the dark cinnamon color featured on a light pink background, they can also have a regular pattern of white dots. These pinks can range from lighter in color to strong, dark variations. Double pinks were often paired with madder or chocolate browns during the height of their popularity in the mid-nineteenth century.*

2 Arrange the units, remaining light squares and triangles, and dark triangles as shown. Sew together to make a block. The block should measure 6½" square, including seam allowances. Repeat to make 53 blocks.

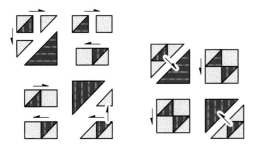

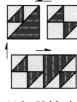

Make 53 blocks,
6½" × 6½".

3 Choose the pieces for one half block. Refer to step 1 of "Making the Blocks" on page 64 to make four half-square-triangle units (you'll use three and set one aside for the pieced border). Lay out the units with the light and dark triangles as shown. Sew together to make one half block. Repeat to make six half blocks.

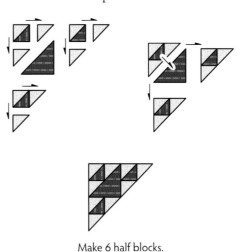

Make 6 half blocks.

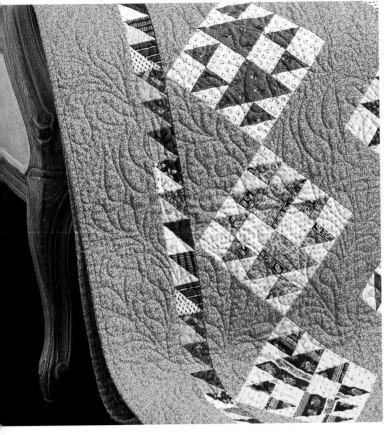

# assembling the quilt top

1 Referring to the diagram below, arrange the blocks, half blocks, pink side setting triangles, and pink corner setting triangles in seven rows: four rows of eight blocks and three rows of seven blocks and two half blocks. Sew triangles to each side of a block, and then sew the block units together to make rows. Each row should measure 9" × 68½", including seam allowances.

Make 4 rows, 9" × 68½".

Make 3 rows, 9" × 68½".

2 Sew the rows together to make the quilt top. The top should measure 60" × 68½", including seam allowances.

# adding the borders

1 Refer to step 1 on page 64 to make 170 assorted half-square-triangle units using the light and dark 2½" squares; the units should measure 2" square, including seam allowances. Add the six half-square-triangle units that were set aside earlier so that you have 176 total.

2 Choose 46 assorted half-square-triangle units and sew them together. Trim ½" from each end of the border to fit the sides of the quilt top. Repeat to make two. Each side border should measure 2" × 68½", including seam allowances. Sew the borders to opposite sides of the quilt top.

3 Choose 42 assorted half-square-triangle units and sew them together, sewing the top-left and bottom-right units so the dark triangles face a different direction. Repeat to make two. Trim ¼" from each end of both borders. The top and bottom borders should

each measure 2" × 63", including seam allowances. Sew to the top and bottom of the quilt. The quilt top should measure 63" × 71½", including seam allowances.

4 Sew together the pink 4½"-wide strips end to end. From the pieced strip, cut two 71½"-long strips and two 71"-long strips. Sew the 71½"-long strips to opposite sides of the quilt top. Sew the 71"-long strips to the top and bottom of the quilt top. The quilt top should measure 71" × 79½".

## finishing the quilt

For help with any of the following finishing steps, visit ShopMartingale.com/HowtoQuilt for instructions.

1 Layer the quilt top, batting, and backing. Baste the layers together. Quilt by hand or machine. The quilt shown is machine quilted using an allover feather pattern.

2 Use the pink 2½"-wide strips to make the binding; attach the binding to the quilt.

## SO MANY HALF-SQUARE TRIANGLES!

*I love pieced borders but I don't love sewing a lot of little pieces. Thank goodness there are easy ways to make half-square-triangle units in multiples. I like to use triangle papers when I have to make a lot of half-square triangles. Follow the directions on the papers to make multiple units at once. Several different manufacturers offer triangle papers; experiment to find your favorite. For this quilt, you need 2" finished triangle papers. Your sewing life just got easier!*

Quilt assembly

# Confetti

*Scrappy Nine Patch blocks are bright and festive–like confetti! Inspired by an antique Pennsylvanian quilt I saw at a quilt study group, my version uses both double pink and chrome yellow. The pieced border features flying geese to continue the festive look. Thanks to my friends Jo and Diane for a Nine Patch block exchange–it provided me a lot of scrappiness for the quilt.*

## materials

*Yardage is based on 42"-wide fabric.*

⅛ yard *each* of 18 assorted light prints for blocks

⅛ yard *each* of 18 assorted dark prints for blocks

1⅜ yards of double pink print for blocks and pieced outer border

2⅜ yards of chrome yellow print for blocks, borders, and binding

3⅓ yards of fabric for backing

60" × 73" piece of batting

### TOXIC YELLOWS

*Chrome yellow fabrics were popular in the early to middle 1800s. Like many of the gold fabrics of the era, chrome yellow fabrics were created with quercitron, a dye made from the bark of the Eastern Black Oak, which was mixed with lead chromate, a toxic substance. Chrome fabrics often featured black or red design details.*

## cutting

*All measurements include ¼"-wide seam allowances.*

**From *each* of the assorted light prints, cut:**
✦ 3 strips, 1¼" × 42" (54 total)

**From *each* of the assorted dark prints, cut:**
✦ 3 strips, 1¼" × 42" (54 total)

**From the double pink print, cut:**
✦ 10 strips, 2¾" × 42"; crosscut into 128 squares, 2¾" × 2¾"
✦ 4 strips, 4½" × 42"; crosscut into 54 rectangles, 2½" × 4½"

**From the chrome yellow print, cut:**
✦ 12 strips, 2¾" × 42"; crosscut into 155 squares, 2¾" × 2¾"
✦ 6 strips, 1¼" × 42"
✦ 15 strips, 2½" × 42"; crosscut 8 of the strips into:
    108 squares, 2½" × 2½"
    4 rectangles, 2½" × 3⅝"
    4 rectangles, ⅞" × 2½"

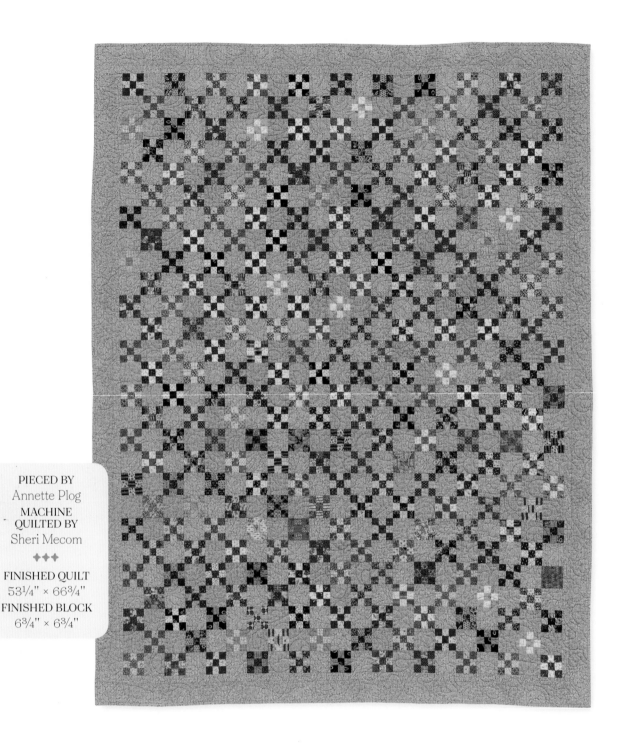

PIECED BY
Annette Plog
MACHINE
QUILTED BY
Sheri Mecom
✦✦✦
FINISHED QUILT
53¼" × 66¾"
FINISHED BLOCK
6¾" × 6¾"

## making the blocks

Use a ¼" seam allowance. Press all seam allowances as indicated by the arrows in the illustrations.

1 Sew together two matching dark strips and one light strip as shown to make strip set A. Crosscut the strip set into 32 A segments that measure 1¼" × 2¾", including seam allowances.

1¼"

Make 1 strip set A, 2¾" × 42".
Cut 32 segments, 1¼" × 2¾".

2 Using the same light and dark prints, sew together two light strips and one dark strip to make strip set B. Crosscut the strip set into 16 B segments that measure 1¼" × 2¾", including seam allowances.

1¼"

Make 1 strip set B, 2¾" × 42".
Cut 16 segments, 1¼" × 2¾".

3 Sew together two A segments and one B segment to make a nine-patch unit. Repeat to make 16 matching units that measure 2¾" square, including seam allowances.

A  B  A

Make 16 matching units,
2¾" × 2¾".

4 Repeat to make a total of 288 nine-patch units (four will be extra).

5 Arrange five assorted nine-patch units and four pink 2¾" squares in three rows as shown. Sew the pieces into rows; join the rows to make a pink Double Nine Patch block that measures 7¼" square, including seam allowances. Make 32 pink Double Nine Patch blocks.

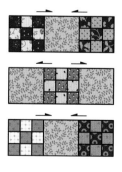 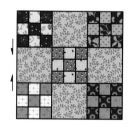

Make 32 blocks,
7¼" × 7¼".

6 Arrange four assorted nine-patch units and five yellow 2¾" squares in three rows as shown. Sew the pieces into rows; join the rows to make a yellow Double Nine Patch block that measures 7¼" square, including seam allowances. Make 31 yellow Double Nine Patch blocks.

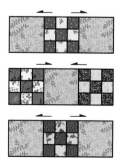 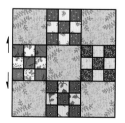

Make 31 blocks,
7¼" × 7¼".

# assembling the quilt top

1. Refer to the quilt assembly diagram below to arrange the pink and yellow blocks alternately in nine rows of seven blocks each. Sew the blocks together in rows. Join the rows to make a quilt top that measures 47¾" × 61¼", including seam allowances.

2. Join the yellow 1¼" × 42" strips end to end to make one long strip. From the pieced strip, cut two 1¼" × 61¼" strips and two 1¼" × 49¼" strips for the inner border. Sew the 1¼" × 61¼" strips to opposite sides of the quilt top. Sew the 1¼" × 49¼" strips to the top and bottom of the quilt top. The quilt top should measure 49¼" × 62¾", including seam allowances.

3. Draw a diagonal line from corner to corner on the wrong side of the yellow 2½" squares. Layer a square on one end of a pink 2½" × 4½" rectangle, right sides together. Sew on the drawn line. Trim ¼" from the drawn line and flip the corner up. Repeat on the other end of the pink rectangle to make a flying-geese unit that measures 2½" × 4½", including seam allowances. Make 54 flying-geese units.

Make 54 units, 2½" × 4½".

4. Sew 12 flying-geese units end to end. Sew a yellow ⅞" × 2½" rectangle to each end to make a pieced border that measures 2½" × 49¼", including seam allowances. Make two. Sew to the top and bottom of the quilt top.

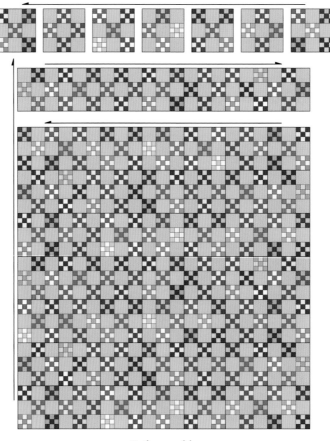

Quilt assembly

5 Sew 15 flying-geese units end to end. Sew a yellow 2½" × 3⅝" rectangle to each end to make a pieced border that measures 2½" × 66¾", including seam allowances. Make two. Sew to opposite sides of the quilt top. The quilt top should measure 53¼" × 66¾".

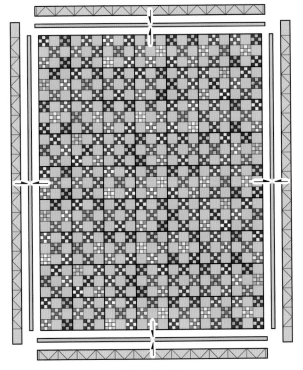

Adding borders

# finishing the quilt

For help with any of the following finishing steps, visit ShopMartingale.com/HowtoQuilt for downloadable instructions.

1 Layer the quilt top, batting, and backing. Baste the layers together.

2 Quilt by hand or machine. The quilt shown is machine quilted using an allover feather pattern.

3 Use the yellow 2½"-wide strips to make the binding; attach the binding to the quilt.

## VINTAGE BATTING

*Don't overlook the batting when re-creating vintage quilts. I love using thin, 100% cotton batting. It's easy to hand quilt, remains flat, and shrinks up to ½" all over. The shrinkage puckers the quilting and gives an antique look. The tighter the quilting, the older the quilt will look.*

# World's Fair

*Many quilt blocks were created to commemorate historical events, and the World's Fair block (a Bear's Paw variation) was probably designed to honor the World's Fair held in Philadelphia in 1876. My friend Marilyn discovered an incredible antique quilt, and we couldn't wait to re-create it. Because of the individuality of each block, I suggest you make one block at a time. The blocks are large and require some appliqué, but they're well worth the time–the results are stunning.*

## materials

*Yardage is based on 42"-wide fabric.*

2⅝ yards *total* of assorted light prints for blocks

3⅛ yards *total* of assorted medium and dark prints for blocks (collectively referred to as "dark")

2 yards of poison green print for sashing, border, and binding

3½ yards of fabric for backing

62" × 79" piece of batting

Template plastic

## cutting

*All measurements include ¼"-wide seam allowances. Each block in this quilt is different. I suggest you cut and sew 1 block at a time. Look at the different blocks, and you'll see different combinations and placement of the light and dark prints. As you cut, vary the values and colors as desired.*

### CUTTING FOR 1 BLOCK (Cut 12 total.)

**From the assorted light prints, cut:**
+ 2 matching squares, 6" × 6"
+ 16 matching squares, 2¼" × 2¼"
+ 4 matching rectangles, 1¾" × 6¾"
+ 6 assorted squares, 1¾" × 1¾"

**From the assorted dark prints, cut:**
+ 2 matching squares, 6" × 6"
+ 4 matching squares, 3½" × 3½"
+ 16 matching squares, 2¼" × 2¼"
+ 4 matching rectangles, 1¾" × 6¾"
+ 2 different squares, 1¾" × 1¾"

### CUTTING FOR CORNERSTONES, SASHING, BORDER, AND BINDING

**From the assorted light and dark prints, cut:**
+ 12 matching sets of 2 squares, 1¾" × 1¾" (24 total)

**From the green print, cut:**
+ 16 strips, 3" × 42"; crosscut 9 of the strips into 17 rectangles, 3" × 15½"
+ 7 strips, 2½" × 42"

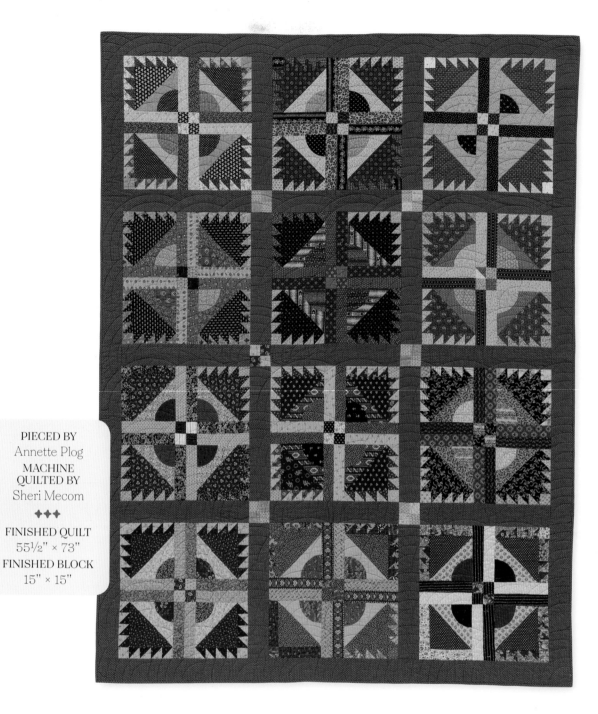

PIECED BY
Annette Plog
MACHINE
QUILTED BY
Sheri Mecom
◆◆◆
FINISHED QUILT
55½" × 73"
FINISHED BLOCK
15" × 15"

# making the blocks

Use a ¼" seam allowance. Press all seam allowances as indicated by the arrows in the illustrations.

1 Using the pieces cut for one block, draw a diagonal line from corner to corner on the wrong side of a light 6" square and layer it on top of a dark 6" square, right sides together. Sew ¼" from both sides of the drawn line. Cut on the line to yield two half-square-triangle units. Trim the units to 5½" square, including seam allowances. Repeat to make four units.

Make 4 units,
5½" × 5½".

2 Make a plastic template using the quarter-circle pattern on page 79. Cut out a quarter circle using the template and a dark 3½" square. Appliqué the quarter circle to the light half of a half-square-triangle unit using your favorite technique. Make four matching appliqué units that measure 5½" square, including seam allowances.

Make 4 appliqué units,
5½" × 5½".

3 Repeat step 1 with the light and dark 2¼" squares. Trim the units to 1¾" square, including seam allowances. Make 32 units.

Make 32 units,
1¾" × 1¾".

4 Join four units from step 3; sew them to one edge of an appliqué unit. Join four units from step 3 and a light 1¾" square. Sew to the adjacent edge of the appliqué unit to make a unit that measures 6¾" square, including seam allowances. Make four matching units.

 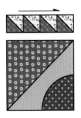 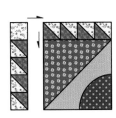

Make 4 units,
6¾" × 6¾".

## KILLER GREEN DYE

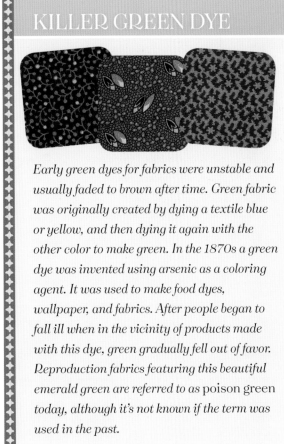

*Early green dyes for fabrics were unstable and usually faded to brown after time. Green fabric was originally created by dying a textile blue or yellow, and then dying it again with the other color to make green. In the 1870s a green dye was invented using arsenic as a coloring agent. It was used to make food dyes, wallpaper, and fabrics. After people began to fall ill when in the vicinity of products made with this dye, green gradually fell out of favor. Reproduction fabrics featuring this beautiful emerald green are referred to as poison green today, although it's not known if the term was used in the past.*

## GOT LEFTOVER BLOCKS?

*When making quilts, you might have leftover blocks that aren't used in the final quilt, such as sample blocks or extra blocks from an exchange. Many quilters use the leftover blocks, called* orphan blocks, *in other quilts. Some quilters will piece the blocks into the backing of the quilt. I had a few blocks left over after making World's Fair, and I used one of my favorites as a quilt label. It lists the name of the quilt, the date completed, and the names of my fellow quilters who donated blocks for the quilt. It's a wonderful way to honor my quilting friends and pass on the history to a future generation!*

5   Join two light and two dark 1¾" squares, alternating them to make a four-patch unit. The unit should measure 3" square, including seam allowances.

Make 1 four-patch unit,
3" × 3".

6   Lay out the stitched units with four light and four dark rectangles in three rows as shown. Sew the pieces into rows; join the rows to make a block. The block should measure 15½" square, including seam allowances. Repeat to make a total of 12 blocks.

       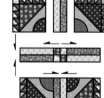

Make 12 blocks,
15½" × 15½".

## assembling the quilt top

1   Referring to step 5 of "Making the Blocks" on page 78 as needed, use the assorted 1¾" squares to make six scrappy four-patch units for cornerstones.

2   Referring to the quilt assembly diagram on page 79, sew together three blocks and two green 3" × 15½" rectangles to make a block row. Make four block rows that measure 15½" × 50½", including seam allowances.

3   Sew three green 3" × 15½" rectangles and two cornerstones together to make a sashing row. Make three sashing rows that measure 3" × 50½", including seam allowances.

4   Sew the block and sashing rows together. The quilt top should measure 50½" × 68", including seam allowances.

5 Sew together the green 3" × 42" strips to make one long strip. Cut this strip into two 3" × 68" strips; sew them to opposite sides of the quilt top. Cut two more strips, 3" × 55½", and sew them to the top and bottom of the quilt top. The quilt top should measure 55½" × 73".

## finishing the quilt

For help with any of the following finishing steps, visit ShopMartingale.com/HowtoQuilt for downloadable instructions.

1 Layer the quilt top, batting, and backing. Baste the layers together.

2 Quilt by hand or machine. The quilt shown is machine quilted using an allover fan pattern.

3 Use the green 2½"-wide strips to make the binding; attach the binding to the quilt.

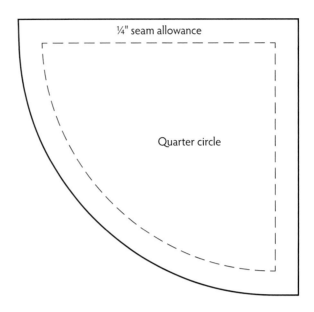
¼" seam allowance

Quarter circle

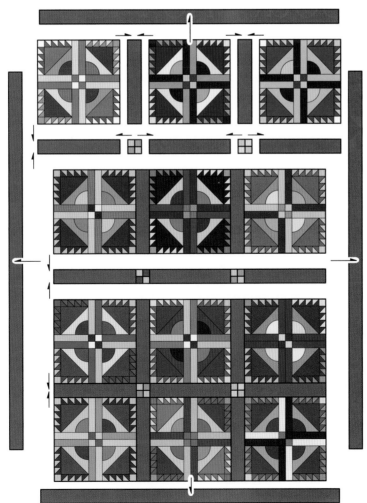
Quilt assembly

## ACKNOWLEDGMENTS

+ Many thanks to my talented and creative stitching groups and friends who love to piece and quilt. They support and inspire my love of traditional fabrics. Many of the quilts featured in this book were made possible through block exchanges that involved these wonderful ladies: Joyce Andrews, Stacey Barrington, Julia Berggren, Pat Boyle, Betsy Chutchian, Betty Edgell, Mary Fornoff, Mary Freeman, Cindy Hansen, Alice Harvey, Arlene Heintz, Janet Henderson, Wanda Hetrick, Karen Hodges, Ann Jernigan, Jean Johnson, Diane Kamego, Sonja Kraus, Jo Massey, Phyllis Masters, Jo Morton, Peggy Morton, Marilyn Mowry, Deb Otto, Diana Petersen, Karen Roxburg, Charlene Seifert, Carol Staehle, Susan Stanley, and Sue Troyan. Your work is forever a part of my most cherished quilts.

+ Many thanks to the Martingale family who held my hand and helped me through this book-writing journey.

+ Thanks to the talented and hard-working machine quilter Sheri Mecom. Her work turned my quilt tops into beautiful creations.

# About the Author

Annette Plog has always loved sewing and antiques, so learning to quilt was the natural extension of those passions. She took her first quilting class in 1987, and grew to love the process of creating quilts for her family. In 1997, Annette was asked to join a group of ladies who loved traditional quilts as much as she did. The group, known as the 19th Century Patchwork Divas, reproduced antique quilts through block exchanges using traditional and reproduction fabrics. While participating in these exchanges, Annette learned valuable lessons in recognizing and dating fabrics. Through block exchanges and reproducing antique quilts, both with the group and on her own, Annette has designed and created quilts that honor the past while providing heirlooms for the future. Annette lectures at local quilt guilds and loves to teach quilting workshops. She is a traditional fabric designer for Windham Fabrics and was honored to be chosen as a 2019 Aurifil Designer. Annette and her husband, Jim, live in north central Texas. They have two grown children, Lauren and David; three grandchildren, Lucy, Joshua, and Riley; and a shepherd mix named Roxy.